Bengt Fredrik Fries

A History of Scandinavian Fishes

Bengt Fredrik Fries

A History of Scandinavian Fishes

ISBN/EAN: 9783337403447

Printed in Europe, USA, Canada, Australia, Japan

Cover: Foto ©ninafisch / pixelio.de

More available books at **www.hansebooks.com**

A HISTORY OF

SCANDINAVIAN FISHES

BY

B. FRIES, C. U. EKSTRÖM, AND C. SUNDEVALL

WITH PLATES

BY

W. von WRIGHT

SECOND EDITION

REVISED AND COMPLETED BY

F. A. SMITT

PLATES

PART I

STOCKHOLM 1892

KUNGL. BOKTRYCKERIET. P. A. NORSTEDT & SÖNER

SCANDINAVIAN FISHES

SECOND EDITION

CONTENTS.

Plate I. 1. Labrus berggylta.
2. Labrus rupestris.
3. Labrus exoletus.
Plate II. 1 & 2. Labrus mixtus.
3. Labrus melops.
Plate III. 1. Perca fluviatilis.
2. Stizostedium lucioperca.
3. Acerina cernua.
Plate IV. 1. Mullus barbatus.
2. Sebastes marinus.
3. Trachinus draco.
Plate V. 1. Agonus cataphractus.
2. Scomber scombrus.
3. Caranx trachurus.
Plate VI. 1. Brama Raii.
2. Cottus quadricornis.
Plate VII. 1. Cottus quadricornis.
2 & 3. Cottus bubalis.
Plate VIII. 1. Cottus gobio.
2 & 3. Cottus scorpius.
Plate IX. 1. Xiphias gladius.
2. Zeus faber.
Plate X. 1. Batrachus didactylus.
2. Lophius piscatorius.
3. Antennarius histrio.
Plate XI. 1. Trigla gurnardus.
2 & 3. Chirolophis galerita.
4. Lumpenus maculatus.
5. Lumpenus lampretiformis.
6. Pholis gunnellus.
Plate XII. 1. Zoarces viviparus.
2. Anarrhichas lupus.
3-5. Gobius niger.
Plate XIII. 1. Anarrhichas minor.
2. Anarrhichas latifrons.
3 & 4. Gobius flavescens.
5. Gobius niceps.
6. Gobius pictus.
7. Gobius minutus.
8 & 9. Aphya minuta.
Plate XIV. Callionymus lyra.

Plate XV. 1. Callionymus maculatus.
2-6. Cyclogaster Montagui.
7-10. Cyclogaster liparis.
11. Mugil chelo.
Plate XVI. Cyclopterus lumpus.
Plate XVII. 1 & 2. Hippoglossus vulgaris.
3. Drepanopsetta platessoides.
Plate XVIII. 1. Bothus maximus.
2. Bothus rhombus.
Plate XIX. 1. Scophthalmus norvegicus.
2. Zeugopterus punctatus.
3. Pleuronectes cynoglossus.
4. Arnoglossus latorna.
Plate XX. 1. Pleuronectes microcephalus.
2. Solea vulgaris.
3. Pleuronectes limanda.
Plate XXI. 1. Pleuronectes flesus.
2. Pleuronectes platessa.
Plate XXII. 1. Gadus aeglefinus.
2 & 3. Gadus callarias.
Plate XXIII, A. 1. Gadus ogac.
2. Gadus luscus.
3. Gadus graellsii.
Plate XXIII. 1. Gadus callarias.
2. Gadus aeglefinus.
3. Rhamphistoma belone.
4. Ammodytes lanceolatus.
Plate XXIV. 1. Gadus merlangus.
2. Gadus minutus.
3. Gadus pollachius.
4. Gadus virens.
Plate XXV. 1. Merlucius merluccius.
2. Phycis blennoides.
3. Raniceps raninus.
4. Brosmius brosme.
Plate XXVI. 1. Lotta lota.
2. Molva molva.
3. Molva dipterygia.
Plate XXVII. 1. Onos cimbrius.
2 & 3. Onos mustela.
4. Orthagoriscus mola.

INDEX.

Pl.	Fig.		Pl.	Fig.
III.	3.	Gobius minutus	XIII.	2.
V.	1.	niger	XII.	3. 5.
XXIII.	4.	pictus	XIII.	6.
XIII.	2.	Hippoglossus vulgaris	XVII.	1 and 2.
XII.	2.	Labrus bergylta	I.	1.
XIII.	1.	exoletus	I.	3.
X.	3.	mixtus	II.	3.
XIII.	8 and 9.	mixtus	II.	1 and 2.
XIX.	4.	rupestris	I.	2.
X.	1.	Lophius piscatorius	X.	2.
XVIII.	1.	Lotta lota	XXVI.	1.
XVIII.	2.	Lumpenus lampretiformis	XI.	5.
VI.	1.	maculatus	XI.	1.
XXV.	4.	Merlangus merlangus	XXV.	1.
XIV.		Molva dipterygia	XXVI.	3.
XV.	1.	molva	XXVI.	2.
V.	3.	Mugil chelo	XV.	11.
XI.	2 and 3.	Mullus barbatus	IV.	1.
VII.	2 and 3.	Onos cimbrius	XXVII.	1.
VIII.	1.	mustela	XXVII.	2 and 3.
VI.	2.	Orthagoriscus mola	XXVII.	4.
VII.	1.	Perca fluviatilis	III.	1.
VIII.	2 and 3.	Pholis gunnellus	XI.	6.
XV.	7 - 10.	Phycis blennoides	XXV.	2.
XV.	2 - 6.	Pleuronectes cynoglossus	XIX.	3.
XVI.		flesus	XXI.	1.
XVII.	3.	limanda	XX.	3.
XII.	1.	microcephalus	XX.	1.
XXII.	1.	platessa	XXI.	2.
XXIII.	2.	Raniceps raninus	XXV.	3.
XXII.	2 and 3.	Rhamphistoma belone	XXIII.	3.
XXIII.	1.	Scomber scombrus	V.	2.
XXII. A.	3.	Scopthalmus norvegicus	XIX.	1.
XXII. A.	2.	Sebastes marinus	IV.	2.
XXIV.	1.	Solea vulgaris	XX.	2.
XXIV.	2.	Stizostedium lucioperca	III.	2.
XXII. A.	1.	Trachinus draco	IV.	3.
XXIV.	3.	Trigla gurnardus	XI.	4.
XXIV.	4.	Xiphias gladius	IX.	1.
XIII.	3 and 4.	Zeugopterus punctatus	XIX.	2.
XIII.	5.	Zeus faber	IX.	2.

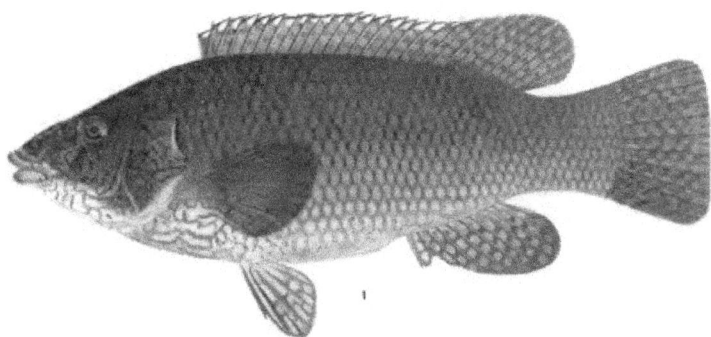

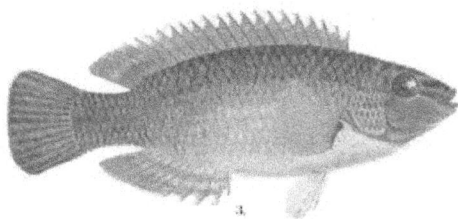

1. Labrus berggylta, 2. Labrus rupestris, 3. Labrus exoletus

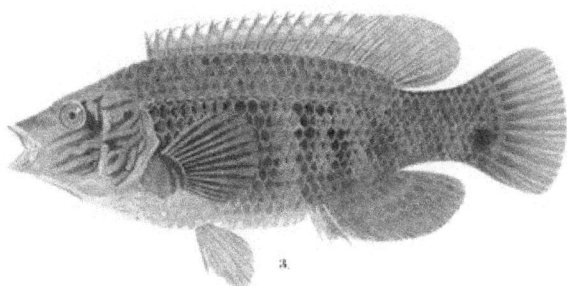

1 et 2. Labrus mixtus, 1 ♂ 2 ♀ ; 3 Labrus melops

1. Perca fluviatilis. 2. Sizostedium lucioperca. 3. Acerina cernua.

1.

2.

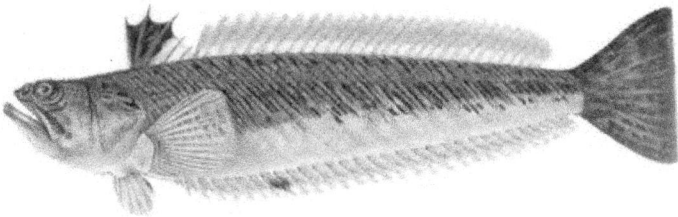

1.

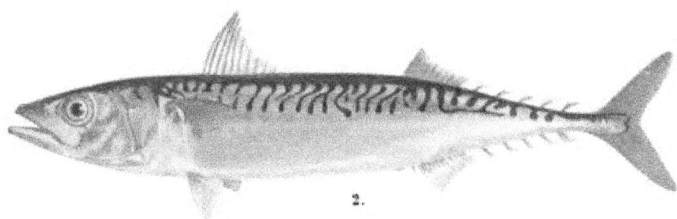

2.

3

2.

1.

1. Brama Ban. 2. Cottus quadricornis.

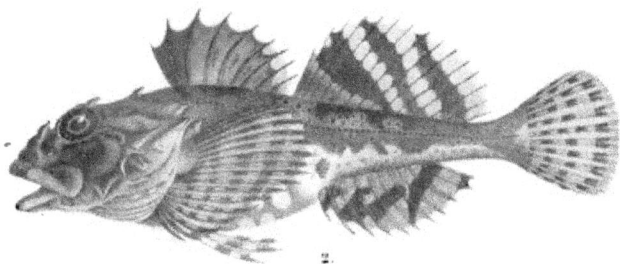

1. Cottus gobio. 2 et 3. Cottus scorpius. 2-♂ 3-♀

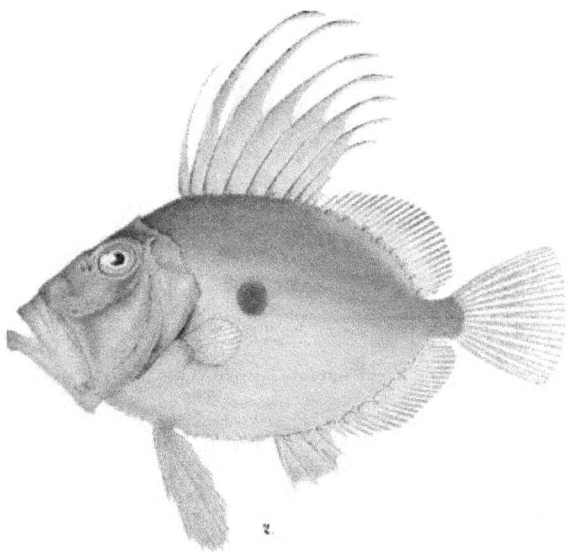

2.

1 Xiphias gladius. 2 Zeus faber

1.Batrachus didactylus, 2. Lophius piscatorius, 3.Antennarius histrio

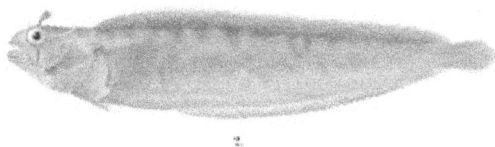

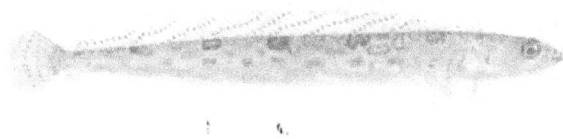

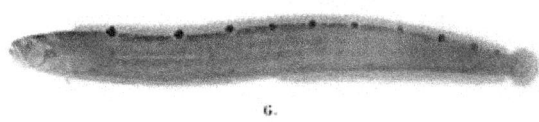

1 Trigla gurnardus. 2 et 3: Chirolophis galerita, 4: Lumpenus maculatus
5: Lumpenus lampretiformis. 6. Pholis gunellus.

1. Enchelyopus viviparus, 2. Anarrhichas lupus 3-5. Gobius niger

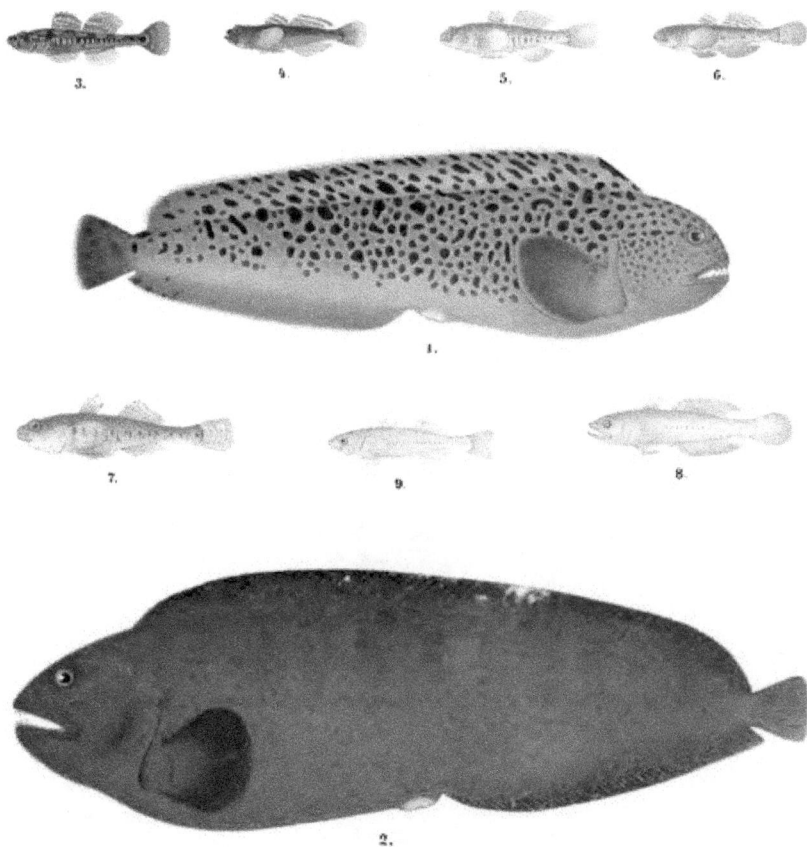

Fig. 1: Anarrhichas minor; 2: Anarrh. latifrons; 3 et 4: Gobius flavescens; 5: Gob. microps; 6: Gob. pictus; 7: Gob. minutus; 8 et 9: Aphya minuta.

1-2, 6-7 Ludwigsen pinx, 3 W. v. Wright pinx, 4-5 Thorsen. apud V. Um. pinx

Pisces Scandinaviæ

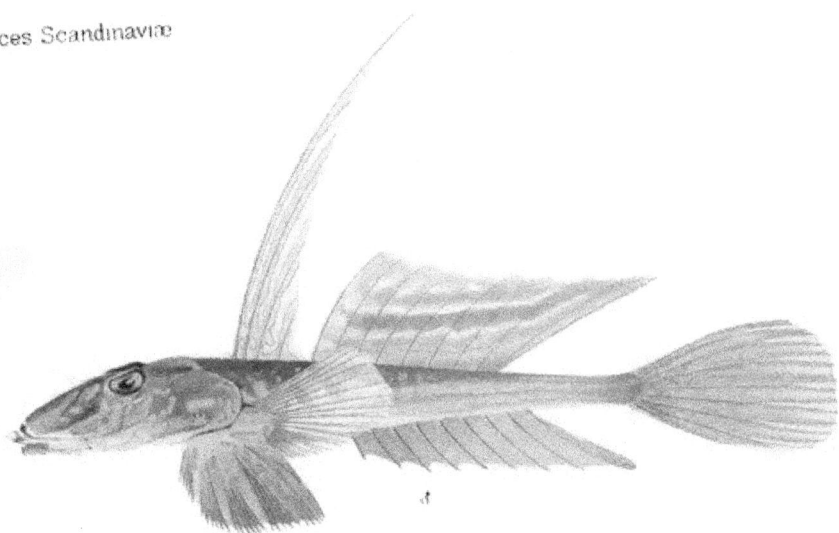

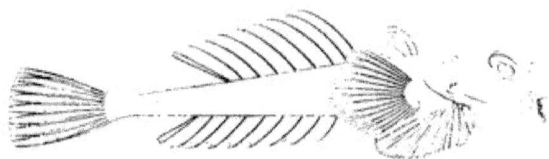

Callionymus lyra.

1.

7.

2.

8.

3.

4.

9.

5.

6.

10.

Cyclopterus lumpus

1 et 2: **Hippoglossus vulgaris**. juv. et sen. 3 Drepanopsetta plattessoides.

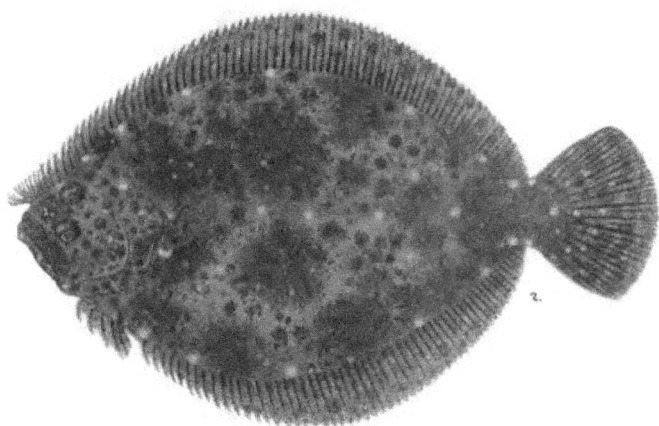

1. Bothus maximus. 2. Bothus rhombus.

1.

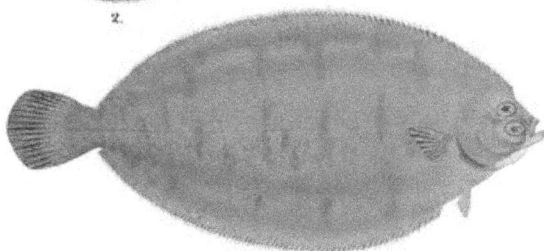

3

4.

1: Scophthalmus norvegicus, 2: Zeugopterus punctatus ju...
3: Pleuronectes cynoglossus, 4: Arnoglossus lateras

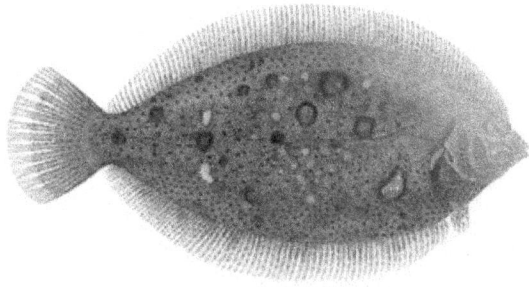

1.

2.

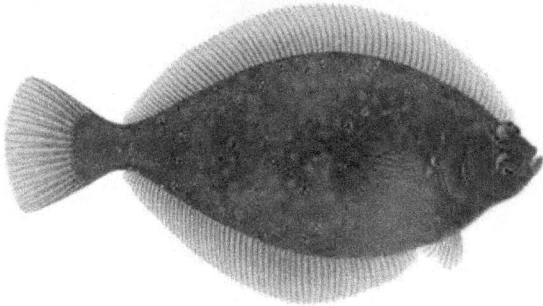

3.

1: Pleuronectes microcephalus, 2: Solea vulgaris, 3: Pleuronectes limanda

1.

ITY

1.

2.

3.

1: Gadus æglefinus, 2 et 3: Gadus callarias

1. Gadus aglae, 2. G. luscus, 3. G. gracilis.

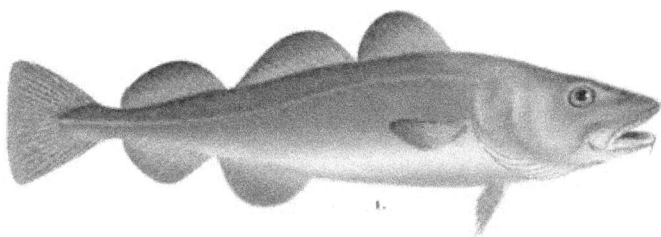

1. ...dus callarias. 2: Gadus æglefinus; 3: Rhamphistoma belone; 4: Ammodytes lanceolatus

1: Gadus merlangus 2: G. minutus 3: G. pollachius 4. G. virens

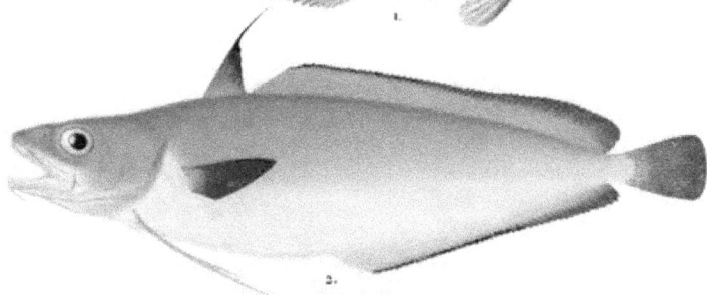

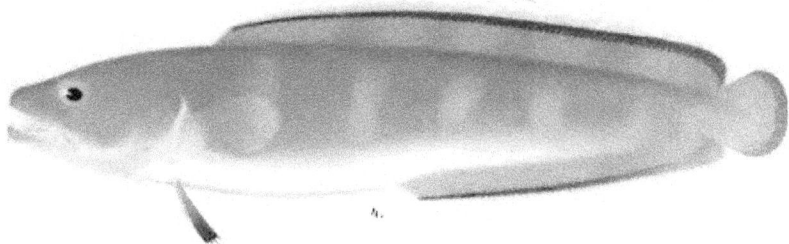

1 Merlucius merluccius. 2 Phycis blennoides; 3: Raniceps raninus. 4: Brosmius brosme

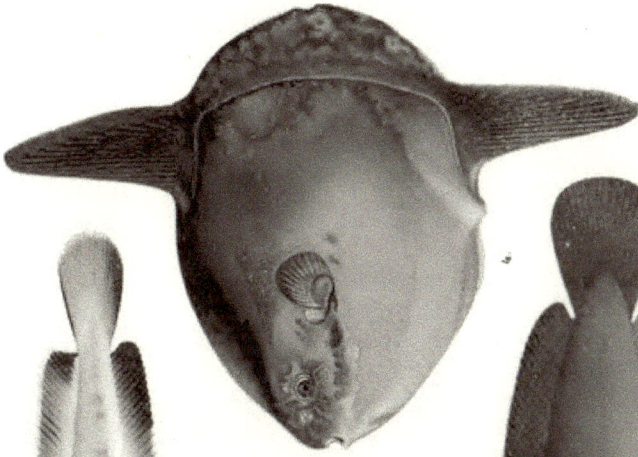